2008

Richard;

Hope that you have many happy times with your new best friend! I know we sometimes wonder why we brought Sierra int[...] [...]ves but I know I don't re[...] [...] of her not in it! Happy Birt[...] [...] glad that you are feeling

Love, Gary & Linda
Sierra too!

Why LABS Do That

Why LABS Do That

A Collection of Curious LABRADOR RETRIEVER Behaviors

Tom Davis

Willow Creek Press

Published by Willow Creek Press
P.O. Box 147, Minocqua, Wisconsin 54548

Editor: Andrea Donner

Library of Congress Cataloging-in-Publication Data
Davis, Tom, 1956-
  Why Labs do that : a collection of curious Labrador retriever behavior /
Tom Davis.
     p. cm.
  ISBN 978-1-59543-422-7 (hardcover : alk. paper)
  1. Labrador retriever--Behavior--Miscellanea. I. Title.
  SF429.L3D38 2008
  636.752'7--dc22
                                    2007046868

Printed in Canada

Contents

Introduction

Most people love their dogs. Labrador people not only love their dogs, they love to talk about them, too, and they'll jump at any chance to do so.

The cab driver, a balding, middle-aged guy a little older than me, was no exception. After I'd given him the address, he asked me what line of work I was in. I told him I was a writer, and that among other things I'd done a number of books about dogs.

That was all the opening he needed. For the rest of the ride from the airport, he talked, and I listened.

"I had a Labrador retriever once. Smartest dog you ever saw…"

He used to own an apple orchard, he said, and his Lab, a female, knew that when he went in to spray the trees with his backpack sprayer she should wait for him at the edge until he came out. "But when I went in to trim limbs with my pruning shears, she'd tag along right beside me. It was nothing I taught her; she just knew the difference.

"And retrieve! You could throw a rock into the pond, and she'd dive for it. Have you ever heard of that? I'm telling you, that dog could do darn near anything…"

He continued in this vein, recounting his Lab's amazing feats, citing examples of her savant-like intelligence, expounding on what a wonderful companion she was not only to him, but to his entire family. "It just about killed us when she died," he said as he stopped in front of the hotel, "and after that we couldn't bring ourselves to get another dog. We knew there'd never be another one like her."

That's the thing about Lab people: To the man, woman, or child, they're all convinced that their dog is one-in-a-million. And why not? A friend of mine, a hunter who's always had Labs, recently decided to branch out and try a pointing breed. Dissatisfied with the progress his pup was making, he called a guy who'd trained several dogs of that breed and asked him what he was doing wrong.

"You're not doing anything wrong," the guy told him. "It's just that you're used to Labs—and they're so smart they're almost human!"

Intelligent, compliant, eager-to-please; playful, affectionate, tolerant; loyal, devoted, courageous: When you add the qualities of its mind and disposition to the sterling physical gifts bred into it since its direct ancestor, the St. Hubert's hound, proved itself the premier all-around hunting dog in renaissance Europe, it's pretty easy to understand why the Labrador retriever is far-and-away the most popular breed in America. The Lab that happily goes for walks and rides in the car and fetches tennis balls in the backyard may never have to break ice and bust through cattails to retrieve a mallard—but it could.

With the proper training, chances are it could also lead the blind, serve the disabled, detect drugs or other contraband, comfort the ill, lonely, or bereaved… the list of the Lab's abilities goes on (and on, and on). About the only chink in the Lab's armor, in fact (not counting the "normal" canine behaviors that appall us prissy humans), is a tendency towards gluttony.

Hey, nobody's perfect—but the Labrador retriever comes awfully close.

Tom Davis
Green Bay, Wisconsin

Why Do Labrador Retrievers Retrieve?

I once had the pleasure of watching Candlewoods Tanks A Lot, one of two dogs in history to win three National Retriever Championships, during a training session. Mike Lardy set up a fiendishly difficult test for her—but she breezed through it as if it were child's play. You could almost hear her saying "Can't you give me something *hard* to do?"

Just as impressive, though, was how eager Lottie remained, after her "work day" was done, to retrieve *something*. What mattered to her was the act, not the object; she'd have been as happy fetching sticks as ducks. The desire to retrieve burned so hot in her that it bordered on a physiological need—if not an outright obsession. But then, given that the Labrador's immediate predecessor, the St. John's dog (also known as the Newfoundland water dog), was expected to dive into the North Atlantic to retrieve fish, the breed clearly had a leg up in this department to begin with.

Of course, that's exactly the point: What distinguishes the Lab from other breeds isn't the inclination to retrieve per se but the *degree of desire*. All dogs have some retrieving instinct, a genetic inheritance from their wolf ancestors. When Mama Wolf picks up a fugitive pup by the scruff of the neck and returns him to the den, she's retrieving; ditto when she brings small prey animals (or pieces of larger ones) to the pups for dinner. Humans eventually recognized that this behavior could be useful to them, and through the agency of selective breeding developed dogs in which this was the dominant and even definitive characteristic—hence the retrieving Superdog that is the modern Labrador.

Why Do Labs Have Such Good Noses?

Somebody once observed that writing about music is like "dancing about architecture." It's an act of interpretation; no matter how rich the vocabulary at your disposal, words don't compare to the experience of actually *hearing the music*.

Writing about the canine sense of smell—"olfaction" if you want to get technical—poses much the same paradox. We can marvel at our Labs' ability to sniff out a mallard in the swampy funk of a cattail marsh, detect the plastic-wrapped cocaine hidden in the belly of a tuna, or pinpoint the location of a body buried beneath tons of rubble. And when the scientists say that our dogs are capable of discerning concentrations of odors in the parts-per-billion range, we can pretend to understand what those numbers really signify. But we still have only the crudest, must rudimentary picture of the brilliant, complex, and infinitely variegated world the Lab's nose reveals to it.

The problem is that because we have noses, too, we invariably try to compare ours to theirs. You know, "The dog's sense of smell is 1,000 times better than ours" or some such thing. To be sure, Labs boast a lot more physiology devoted to smelling than we do: 200-220 million "scent receptors" (as opposed to our paltry five million); nasal membranes that unfolded would be the size of a handkerchief (ours would be the size of a postage stamp); a specialized structure in the roof of the mouth known as Jacobson's organ that enables them to taste what they smell; olfactory bulbs (the "translator stations" between the nose and the brain) that are four times the size of ours, and on and on.

The bottom line is that the canine sense of smell is so vastly superior to ours that the only valid and meaningful comparison is to our sense of sight. Think of it this way: Labs may look with their eyes—but they see with their noses.

Why Are Labs So Trainable?

A good case can be made that the Lab is the most trainable of all purebred dogs. Or, if you want to hedge your bet a little, you could argue that at the very least no breed is *more* trainable. And when you hitch this trainability to the Lab's robust physique, rugged constitution, even temperament, and all-around athleticism, you get a dog whose ability to perform multiple tasks, from fetching ducks to serving people with disabilities, is unsurpassed.

Intelligence, of course, is a prerequisite to trainability, and the Lab's intelligence is a given. Way back in 1861, one Lambert de Boilieu remarked that the Labrador "when well taught understands, almost as well as any Christian biped, what you say to him."

What may be even more important to this equation, though, is the happily subservient *receptivity* to training known as "eagerness to please." It's this quality that, alloyed with intelligence, makes the Lab both *easily* trainable, in the sense of obediently accepting commands, and *highly* trainable, in the sense of having the capacity to carry out complex tasks. Labs also ring the bell in what behavioral scientists call "working memory," which is what enables them, for example, to remember where one duck (or several) fell while they're in the act of retrieving another. The more and better a dog remembers, the more and quicker it's able to learn.

It comes back to the fact that for hundreds of years Labs and their progenitors have always had jobs to do—jobs that required them to be attentive and obedient to their human partners. Selectively breeding the individuals who exemplified these traits not only perpetuated them in the Labrador line, but enhanced them to the outstanding degree we see today.

Why Do Labs Love to Chase Things?

All dogs, to one degree or another, are inclined to chase. I like to say that when you scratch a dog (even as "civilized" a dog as the Lab) you find a wolf, and the wolf's instinctive response to motion—and in particular to anything that seems to be fleeing (a prey animal, for example)—is to go after it. Over the millennia, as the individuals that chased first and asked questions later came up sevens in the evolutionary crapshoot, this behavior, like just about every other behavior that contributed to survival, was hard-wired into the genetic motherboard. Animal ethologists call it "prey chase drive."

Certainly wolves, and therefore dogs, have some control over this impulse (unlike weasels, who literally can't help themselves and, if they get into the henhouse, will continue killing chickens until every last one is dead, or has at least stopped moving).

As a hunting breed—or more officially, a member of the "sporting group"—the Lab has a comparatively high prey chase drive. This, again, is the result of dozens of generations of selective breeding. The desire to retrieve, in fact, can be viewed as a manifestation of this drive: Before a Lab retrieves an object is has to catch it, essentially, and in order to catch it, it has to chase it. Where the Lab differs from the wolf (and the weasel) is that instead of killing what it catches, it retrieves it. And, if it happens to be a gamebird, *you* get to eat it. This is why retrieving, like pointing and even herding, is known as an "inhibitory behavior": It stops short of its natural outcome and results instead in an outcome useful to humans.

It's as simple as this: As long as Labs are bred to retrieve, they're going to chase things. It's our job as their owners to make sure they learn to chase the right things.

Why Do Labs Love Water and Swimming?

I've already alluded to the fact that the Lab's immediate predecessor, the St. John's dog, was expected to retrieve fish. You can credit trainability, eagerness-to-please, and mental toughness all you want, but unless a dog has the physical equipment to handle icy water, it's not likely to make the cut on the cod-fetching team. The very name "Labrador," first used to describe these dogs in 1814, is itself instructive, Labrador having been famously described by the explorer John Cabot as "the land that God gave Cain."

Because the Lab was developed for (and shaped by) extreme conditions, chief among them icy water, its design incorporates a number of specialized elements. Its coat, for starters. Short, slick, and superbly water-repellant, with an outer "shell" of glossy guard hairs and a "lining" of dense underfur, it affords a combination of high protection and low maintenance. The Lab is also endowed with a generous layer of subcutaneous fat, which serves to further insulate it from the effects of the cold and, I suspect, also plays a role in creating buoyancy in the water.

In addition, the Lab boasts some pretty refined swimgear. Its feet have more "webbing" between the toes than most breeds. Then there's the distinctive "otter" tail, the primary purpose of which is to serve as a rudder (but which also makes a stout emergency handle if your boat capsizes in the middle of a storm-roiled lake and your only hope for survival is to grab on and let your Lab tow you to shore).

Beyond these adaptations, most Labs just seem to enjoy the heck out of swimming, splashing around, and frolicking in the water. They have a natural affinity for the stuff, a gravitational attraction that I speculate has been bred into them as the individuals who displayed the most zest for water work were rewarded with the opportunity to reproduce.

Why Do Labs Wolf Their Food and Eat So Much of It?

Of the Lab's many claims to fame, one of the more dubious is that it may well be the champion chowhound. The immortal words of Beldar Conehead—"Let us consume mass quantities"—are its mantra; Temple Grandin, the renowned animal behaviorist, goes so far as to call the Lab a "compulsive overeater." But it's really just doing what comes naturally.

During the past decade or so a fierce debate has raged over how recently, or not, the "transition" from wolf to dog occurred. The archaeological evidence puts dogs in the camps of Stone Age man 15,000 years ago. But the DNA-unravelers contend that the dog-wolf "split" began much earlier—over 100,000 years ago, they say.

Regardless, there's no doubt that the wolf existed in largely the same form it does today for thousands of years before the dog made the scene. And during those millennia, as the individuals that ate fast and heartily survived, this behavior became incorporated at the genetic level. It not only enabled the wolf to succeed within the framework of the competitive pack, but to survive during periods when prey was hard to come by.

In other words, the reason wolves feast gluttonously whenever the opportunity arises—hence the metaphor "wolfing food"—is that it's their built-in hedge against famine. You never know, in the wild, when your next meal's coming.

Somewhere deep in your Lab's psyche, then—near the place where the wolf still howls—a part of it worries that something bigger and badder is going to steal its food. This same part also refuses to take its next meal for granted, despite the fact that it's probably never missed or been denied one.

And so your Lab eats as if there's no tomorrow.

Why Do Labs Dislike the Heat and Pant So Much?

An art as well as a science, dog breeding involves compromise and the making of "either/or" decisions. In the case of the Lab, the watermen and sportsmen who developed it put a premium on its ability to perform in cold, wet conditions. Given this priority, they gave essentially no thought to how well their dogs could handle the heat.

The Lab suffers more than most in hot weather. Size is one reason. Because of the comparatively low ratio of surface area (i.e., skin), which dissipates heat, to internal area, which generates it, larger breeds like the Lab feel the heat sooner and more acutely than smaller breeds do. Then there's that layer of fat, which insulates against the cold and therefore *conserves* heat—great on a December duck hunt but not so good in the "dog days" of summer.

Many Labs are further handicapped by their color. If you recall Physics 101, you know that dark colors absorb light, thus creating heat, while light colors reflect it. The ramifications for a black or chocolate Lab are obvious.

The reason Labs pant is that, as with all dogs, it's their primary means of maintaining normal body temperature (around 101°F). The rapid movement of air across the moist membranes of the mouth, throat, and tongue causes the moisture on these surfaces to evaporate, thus drawing off heat and cooling the underlying blood vessels. Panting also functions as a rudimentary heat exchange, warmer air going out, cooler air coming in. Alas, as more than one authority has noted, it's an "inefficient" system, easily overwhelmed by high temperatures and/or exertion. This is why "outside" Labs should always have access to shade and water, why exercise in the heat of the day should be limited, and why you should never leave a Lab, or any other dog, unattended and locked in a vehicle when it's hot and sunny.

Why Do Labs Have Such Slick, Shiny Coats?

As noted previously, the Lab's coat is one of the canine race's crowning achievements in design and engineering. With a weather-repellant outer shell of glossy, stiff guard hairs intermingled with finer "secondary" hairs and an insulating layer of downlike underfur, it's something like a waxed-cotton jacket laminated to a wool sweater—which, given the places the Lab comes from and what the *people* there wear, is not surprising. It's the original "shake-dry" garment, too, abundantly supplied with natural oil—*sebum*, this is called—that makes water bead up and be easily shed. And, just as importantly, not absorbed, meaning that the Lab doesn't bring half the lake with it into the blind or boat along with the duck. For comparison's sake, the golden retriever's coat retains almost 50 percent more water than the Lab's.

The sebum, of course, along with other oily secretions, is what gives the Lab's coat its slick, shiny appearance. The coat of a black Lab is especially impressive, glinting and shimmering like a raven's wing.

It comes back to the work the Lab and its predecessors were expected to do. The St. John's dog of Newfoundland was first and foremost a water dog, and because form follows function, the individuals who excelled at their jobs had the right "clothes" for it. Some of this was undoubtedly an inheritance from the St. Hubert's hound, the all-purpose hunting breed that found its way to Devon in the southwest of England and from there to the cod fishing grounds of the New World. But there was certainly some "tinkering" that went on; at least one of the early depictions of the Labrador shows a dog with a much longer, setter-like coat. It remained for the gentlemen-sportsmen who assumed custodianship of the breed in the 19th century to refine and perfect the Labrador type—including its incomparable coat.

Why Do Labs Come in Three Colors?

The "primordial" color of the Labrador retriever, of course, is black. It's the color chiefly associated with the St. Hubert's hounds, the St. John's dogs, and the fountainhead Labradors that graced the kennels of Malmesbury, Buccleuch, and Home. As early as 1576, however, it was reported that an occasional St. Hubert's dog "proved white"—which modern authorities interpret to mean "yellow" and point to as evidence that the recessive yellow gene was part of the mix even then. Similarly, a few St. John's dogs are described as "liver," which these days we'd call "chocolate."

In other words, the evidence is good that all three colors have been part of the Lab's genetic palette since the start of the breed. And once the prejudice against any color but black faded away—yellows gained popularity in the 1950s, chocolates in the '70s—it was no trick for breeders to cultivate the recessive genes and produce these colors more-or-less on demand. The rusty hue known as "red fox" is simply the dark end of the yellow spectrum. As for the so-called "silver" color phase, some argue that it's a chocolate variant and therefore perfectly legitimate—and some argue that it's the result of a midnight tryst between a Lab and Weimaraner.

For the record, here's what you can expect to get, theoretically, from the six possible sire/dam color combinations:

- Black x Black: all
- Black x Yellow: all
- Black x Chocolate: all
- Yellow x Yellow: yellow
- Yellow x Chocolate: all
- Choc. x Choc.: chocolate, yellow

Behind these six "visible" combinations swirls an astonishing number of *genetic* color combinations: 81, to be precise. Don't ask me how they came up with that figure, because I'd have to start using words like "alleles" and "homozygous."

Why Aren't Labs Multi-Colored?

Actually, a very few Labs *are* multi-colored. They're not dogs of dubious ancestry, either, but the pedigreed, purebred sons and daughters of typical "self-colored" (all one color) parents. Even champion Labs have been known to throw an occasional "mismark," as dogs whose coloration falls outside the official breed standard are called.

Among the common mismarks (relatively speaking) are black or chocolate Labs with tan "points"—eyebrows, muzzles, ears, and paws. Imagine a Gordon setter with a boot camp haircut, and you've got the idea. Then there are "brindled" Labs, whose coats, the hairs literally alternating in color, are remindful of multiple flavors of ice cream swirled together. (Or like a Plott hound, if you know what a Plott hound looks like.) "Mosaics"—yellow Labs with black splotches that may occur anywhere on their body—fall into this category as well.

It's thought that mismarks occur either when both parents contribute a long-buried recessive gene or as the result of a chromosome mutation in the fetal puppy. Functionally, there's nothing wrong with these dogs; for just about any purpose except the show ring or breeding, they're just as fit as any other Lab. They just don't look the way we expect Labs to look—although if anything that makes them even more endearing.

Why Do Labs Enjoy Being Brushed?

Because it feels so deliciously, exquisitely, rapturously good, that's why. While it's true (as we've already established) that Labs have about the most low-maintenance coat in the canine wardrobe, they still go *ga-ga* over a vigorous brushing. I imagine it feels something like a scalp massage feels to us, all tingly and invigorating yet at the same time soothing and almost hypnotically relaxing. It gets the blood flowing to the dermal capillaries, stimulates production of sebum and other secretions conducive to a healthy coat and skin, cleans out the itchy dead hair… Oh, yeah.

It's also the case that a Lab getting brushed is a Lab getting attention, typically from someone whose attention said Lab craves—and what's not to like about that? The basic physical contact is another component of this, along with the brushing motion itself, which some authorities believe stirs puppyhood memories of the dog being licked by its dam.

This is for certain, though: Your brushing muscles will give out long before your Lab's appetite for being brushed does.

Why Do Labs Come in So Many Different Shapes and Sizes?

No species, taken as a whole, exhibits more of what scientists call "morphological variation" than our friend *Canis lupus familiaris*. It strains the imagination to believe that a handbag-sized chihuahua and a Great Dane you could darn near throw a saddle on have essentially the same DNA, but it's a fact. There are no genetic "markers" that distinguish one breed from another.

The point is, a tremendous amount of elasticity is built-in to the dog's raw genetic material—and even within the chunk that defines the Lab there's more than enough stretch for breeders to produce fine-boned 50-pounders that are as light on their feet as ballerinas and massive 100-pounders ("Dreadnaughts," in field trial argot) that'll body-slam anything that gets between them and whatever they've been sent to retrieve.

There are leggy Labs and stocky Labs, Labs with square muzzles and Labs with slender ones, Labs with short, thick tails and Labs with long, springy tails. Like begets like, as they say, and a breeder who wants to produce dogs with specific conformation characteristics can, by carefully choosing the sires and dams, achieve startling results in just two or three generations.

In general, as is the case with many of the sporting breeds, there are two basic Labrador "types": a show type that's generally heavier and blockier in appearance and more ponderous in action, and a field/hunting type that's rangier and more athletic. Some would argue that there's a third type: the British Lab, which is bred primarily for the field but has a more chiseled, "classic" look than its American counterpart.

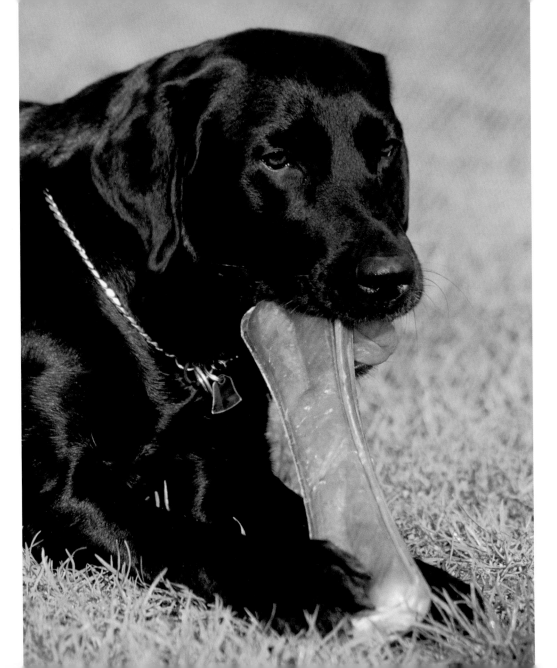

Why Do Labs Love to Chew?

Whenever I watch Roger Federer play tennis, I wonder what it would be like to hold a racquet in my hand and feel what he does. A golf club in the hands of Annika Sorenstam, a baseball bat in the hands of Albert Pujols, a guitar in the hands of Eric Clapton—you get the idea.

Well, if you accept the premise that the dog's mouth serves as its hands, insofar as it's what they use to pick things up, hold them, and carry them around, you can make the case that just as the canine race in general represents "the rest of us," the Labrador (a.k.a. the Ultimate Retriever) represents the Federers and Sorenstams. The virtuosos, in other words, the geniuses, the blessed with respect to the capabilities of their mouths. And because the desire to *employ* their mouths is so powerful—and somewhat indiscriminate—it occasionally lands them in deep doo-doo. "Notorious chewers" is how animal behaviorist Temple Grandin characterizes the Lab, and everyone who's ever owned one has a story to tell about the things his or hers chewed to smithereens: the fancy walnut stock of a prized shotgun, a closetful of designer high-heels, the list goes on and on.

Personally, I'm convinced that the Lab's propensity to chew is connected to the desire to retrieve, a component of which is the desire simply *to feel things in their mouths*. Labs, in fact, are known for being "mouthy," a common example of which is gently grabbing your hand or wrist. Chewing can also be a reflection of boredom, irritation, or some combination thereof—or it could be that Labs chew because it allows them to blow off some emotional steam and safely vent the frustration that builds up from keeping their baser urges in check and serving as role models for the rest of canine society.

Why Do Labs Yip and Twitch When They're Asleep?

Long before scientists confirmed that dogs dream by measuring their brain activity with EEGs, dog folk had no doubt that that's exactly what they were doing when they twitch, jerk, "paddle," yip, woof, and sometimes even growl while they're asleep. If you're a disciple of Freud, who believed that dreams are expressions of repressed desires, it's tempting to imagine that your Lab's dreaming about all the things its "bad self" would love to do: chase cats, bite mailmen, chew on furniture, sneak out for an illicit liaison with the poodle down the block and a celebratory post-tryst howl at the moon. It seems more likely, though, that their dreams are essentially a mirror of their lives. For example, I have no doubt whatsoever that Labs used for hunting dream about flushing pheasants from the burnished autumn fields or vaulting into icy water to retrieve ducks—happy times, indeed.

The phase of sleep in which dogs dream most actively is known as "rapid eye movement" (REM) sleep. It's during REM sleep that dogs twitch and yip. Indeed, brain activity during REM sleep is virtually a dead ringer for fully conscious brain activity, begging the question: Why don't they jump up and start running around instead of merely twitching? The answer is that during REM sleep they're essentially paralyzed. The brainstem sends a message down the spinal cord, activating an "inhibitory pathway," and the large voluntary muscles are "off-line."

As it happens, Labs are among the dozen or so breeds known to suffer from narcolepsy, an affliction that causes them to suddenly fall into REM sleep. Neurologists at Stanford studied narcoleptic Labs to glean crucial insights into the causes of the disease in humans. Leave it to the Lab to find a way, even while fast asleep, to lend a helping paw.

Why Do Labs Have So Much Energy?

Certainly Labs have no monopoly in this department—been around any Jack Russell terriers lately?—and it's also the case that you run into an occasional Lab that's a real sofa spud. (It's not so much that they're innately phlegmatic, typically, as just a bit over-served at the food bowl. You'd be reluctant to move, too, if you were lugging all that excess weight around.)

A Lab that's healthy and fit, however, will keep going long after you've reached the point at which you're ready to plunk your weary bones down in close proximity to your favorite beverage. The Roman dictum *carpe diem*—"Seize the day"—could have been coined with the Labrador in mind; they're unfailingly up for every challenge, eager to make the most of every opportunity. The Lab greets each new dawn the way my grandfather did. "Where's the pool," he'd proclaim to whoever was in earshot, "and what's the record?"

A big part of this, I'm convinced—maybe the biggest part—is attitude. Unencumbered by the existential *angst* that wracks us humans, never feeling that the weight of the world is pressing down on their shoulders, and dwelling neither on the mistakes of the past nor the uncertainties of the future, Labs take every moment as it comes, displaying a zest for life and living that we'd do well to emulate—if we could keep up with them. And that's another thing: In terms of sheer stamina, no human was ever born who, over the long haul, could keep up with a well-conditioned Lab.

Why Do Labs Smile So Much—
or Do They Just Look Like They're Smiling?

If a Lab looks like it's smiling, it's because it is, dammit. What you have to understand is that by molding, shaping, and sculpting the various breeds out of the gob of raw genetic material stamped *Canis lupus familiaris*, man has essentially played God. He has created the dog in his own image—and, in particular, your better breeds of dogs, a list headed up by the Labrador retriever. And just as there's no animal capable of feeling the almost-human range of emotions the dog feels, there's no animal capable of expressing them so power-fully, eloquently, and unmistakably as the dog does (that is, so that even dim-witted *Homo sapiens*, with our dulled senses, cluttered minds, and exaggerated opinions of ourselves, have no trouble recognizing them).

A cynic might argue that this is at least partly a learned behavior, the Lab having figured out that the more it smiles, the more attention, affection, and praise it receives. But this ignores the crucial fact that dogs tend to be very bad at hiding, or even disguising, their true feelings. They're not by nature dissemblers—and Labs, in particular, are exceptionally forthright. They're straight-shooters; what they show is how they feel. The reason they smile so much is that they're happy—happy to be alive, happy to have shelter and food and a "pack" to belong to, happy to be *yours*. It's as pure—and as simple—as that.

Why Do Labs Love to Play?

The reasons Labs are so happy and energetic (see the previous two questions) also help to explain why Labs love to play. But there's something else at work here, too. In his classic book *Upland Passage*, the late Robert F. Jones mused that the Labs he's known "have had a greater sense of fun and retained it longer after puppyhood than any other breed I'm familiar with… In many respects, the most important quality handed down from the St. Hubert's hound through the Newfoundland water dog to the Labrador retriever of today is this unquenchable spirit of playfulness."

Jones argued that there's a direct connection between the Lab's great playfulness and its extraordinary trainability—a contention that matches up perfectly with the latest thinking about what separates dogs from wolves. Genetically they're all but identical; the difference, for the record, has been calculated at 0.2 percent. The wedge, the crucial fulcrum that allowed the dog to split off, is the phenomenon of *neoteny*, a working definition of which is "the retention of juvenile characteristics into adulthood." This is what makes dogs both eminently trainable—"behaviorally plastic" in science-speak—and eternally playful. At a certain level, they never stop being puppies. Think of it this way: There's a bit of Peter Pan in all dogs—and more than most, a *lot* more, in the Lab.

Why Are Labs So Good With Children?

There's no single reason; rather, it's a combination of a number of the qualities Labs are renowned for: even temperament; sweet, equable disposition; that eternal playfulness; their deep, and deeply discerning, intelligence. Most Labs are also very gentle dogs, with a sense of how powerful they are and how much damage they're capable of doing; by the same token, most Labs seem to feel a kind of protective responsibility for *all* the members of their human "pack," kids and adults alike—although, granted, they're probably a bit more protective of the young, whose comparative weakness and vulnerability is an open book to them. As we'll see later, dogs—especially breeds like Labs with a long, uninterrupted history of working closely with humans—excel at "reading" people.

Another factor in this equation is that Labs are one of the few dog breeds classified as "low fear" *and* "low aggression." (Usually a dog that's low in one of these respects is high in the other, and vice-versa.) This translates into a dog that's secure, confident, and emotionally and behaviorally stable, one that's slow to anger and bares its fangs, figuratively and/or literally, only under the most extreme duress. With respect to children, this means that the Lab tends to be exceptionally tolerant. Instead of lashing out, for example, when its ears or tail gets pulled during otherwise "normal" rough-housing, a Lab will typically yip to tell the perpetrator *Hey, that hurts!* and then just move out of harm's way. Or, at most, it'll gently take the offending hand in its mouth and remove it, just as it might remove a puppy that's testing out its new, needle-sharp teeth. This is why the "soft mouth" prized by hunters—the ability to retrieve a gamebird without damaging it—is also something to be desired in a child's canine playmate.

Why Do Labs Crave—and Display—So Much Affection?

It comes back to this concept of neoteny, to the fact that at a fundamental level every dog, and therefore every Lab, is a puppy in an adult's body. (A lot of women would say that that's a pretty good definition of most of the men they know, but let's not go there.) More specifically, every dog, and therefore every Lab, is a *wolf* puppy in an adult's body. And just as the wolf puppy has a deeply rooted need for affirmation and positive reinforcement from its superiors in the hierarchy of the pack, the Lab, throughout its life, craves the attention and affection of the human family that comprises its "pack"—and whose members it perceives as its superiors. Feeling loved, and that it *belongs*, are essential to the Lab's sense of well-being, although some Labs are more needy (or more stoic) in this respect than others.

The thing is, they give as good as they get. Maybe better, even. This is one of the big reasons Labs are such terrific family dogs and all-around companions. They're not shy about showing how they feel; they typically wear their hearts on their sleeves, and if sloppy emotional displays aren't your style you're not, by definition, a Lab person. It's as if they're overwhelmed by gratitude, as if they literally can't help themselves. The affection pours out of them like champagne when the cork pops.

Why Do Labs Enjoy "Kissing" People?

This is a perfect example of what behaviorists call a "positive feedback loop": Your Lab gives you a tentative lick on the face, you respond with delight (although you may grimace, go *phlooey!*, and feign disgust), and your Lab, its behavior reinforced, does it again—with feeling.

Given how profoundly scent-oriented the canine race is in general, my guess is that Labs are initially drawn to our faces because of the intriguing bouquet of aromas emanating from there. Dogs can detect concentrations of odors in the parts-per-billion range, remember, so it doesn't take much to get their attention—a microscopic smear of the chicken cacciatore you had for dinner, a granule of the blueberry muffin you grabbed for breakfast, or pretty much whatever else you've eaten in the previous 24 hours. Dogs seem to enjoy the smell of our breath, too, which is hard to fathom until you recall that dogs (very much including Labs) also like to wallow in roadkill, smear themselves with the vilest goo imaginable, and eat things that'd make the stuff they eat on *Fear Factor* look like pheasant under glass.

Anyway, once they've figured out that this licking deal goes over big, it's all over but the shoutin'. Your Lab will be kissing you for the rest of its days—it's yet another way for them to display affection—and you'll be loving it.

Why Do Labs Sometimes Develop Phobias and Mental Disorders?

Labs, on the whole, are about as psychologically stable a breed as there is—a fact that goes a long way toward explaining their immense popularity. As we've seen, they tend to be highly intelligent, highly trainable dogs, although it'd be a big mistake to assume that every Lab's a canine Rhodes Scholar.

Still, there are some very real afflictions that can compromise a Lab's ability to function "normally." Perhaps the most common is attention-deficit *hyperactivity* disorder. In Labs as in people, this condition makes it difficult for them to focus and stay "on task"— and puts increased demands on the patience of those in charge of training and caring for them. A variety of medical conditions, ranging from joint pain to thyroid imbalance to epilepsy, can also have a significant effect on behavior and overall "mental equilibrium."

Labs sometimes exhibit obsessive-compulsive behaviors as well, such as constant licking or chewing (often on themselves). The current thinking is that these disorders are symptomatic of a biochemical imbalance in the brain. Nor are Labs immune to phobias, one of the most confounding being the fear of thunderstorms. The confounding part is not that "family" Labs can be reduced to quivering, slobbering wrecks by a thunderclap, but that hunting Labs—who are used to the report of a shotgun—seem equally susceptible. Evidence also suggests that dogs may suffer from a canine form of post-traumatic stress disorder. For example, a dog that's shaken up in an auto accident who then refuses to get in the car.

The more aware you are of everything that can go wrong, the more thankful you are that, with Labs, most of the time everything goes right.

Why Do Labs Make Such Good Guide and Service Dogs?

Pretty much all the outstanding qualities we've cited to this point contribute to the Lab's status as the number one choice, overwhelmingly, for guide and service work. Intelligence, trainability, eagerness to please, sound temperament, predisposition to "partner" with people, the ability to focus on the assignment at hand: If you drew up a psychological blueprint of the ideal guide and service dog, it'd look an awful lot like a profile of the Labrador retriever. The Lab's unique combination of low fear and low aggression is another critically important part of the equation; it's what allows the Lab to maintain a cool head in stressful situations, to respond with its training rather than react out of instinct, and to unhesitatingly enter smouldering wreckage and other threatening environments where many dogs would fear to tread.

The Lab's physical qualifications are just as well-matched. Honed by generations of breeding for the field, lake, and marsh, the Lab's robust conformation makes it the quintessential all-around athlete: strong yet agile, big enough but not so big that its size becomes a handicap. The Lab's remarkable stamina serves it well in this respect, too, while its high prey drive, re-directed via training, translates into a relentlessly tenacious search-and-rescue, drug detection, or bomb detection dog. The upshot is that in terms of the ability to do a wide variety of jobs under a wide variety of conditions—and to do them at an extremely high level of competence—the Labrador retriever is simply without peer.

Why Do Labs Hunt Upland Birds as Well as Waterfowl?

It's a little-known fact that one of the keys to the Lab's rise to prominence in the United States—which began in the 1910s (the first Lab was registered with the American Kennel Club in 1917), slowly gained momentum in the 1920s and '30s, and skyrocketed in the years following World War II—was the population explosion of another "import," the ring-necked pheasant. A bird that'd rather run than fly, the pheasant proved a tough customer for the pointers and English setters that were the American sportsman's traditional choices for upland bird hunting. A different kind of gun dog was needed—and in the close-working, cover-crashing Lab, it was found. With a Lab at your side, you could hunt waterfowl at dawn, then, following breakfast and a change of clothes, spend the rest of the day chasing pheasants or other upland birds.

The interesting thing is that no one really suspected that the Lab was as versatile a hunter as it's turned out to be, especially with the "all-purpose" legacy of the St. Hubert's hound unknown until fairly recently. During the breed's formative period in the 19th and early 20th centuries it was used almost exclusively as a "non-slip" retriever, a dog that sat or heeled at its handler's side until turned loose—"slipped"—to make a retrieve. But with its keen nose, high prey chase drive, and ability to quickly grasp what's expected of it, the Lab took to pheasant hunting in about the time it takes to yell "Rooster!"

Why Do Labs Dominate Retrieving Competitions?

The first field trial for retrievers in the United States was held in 1931, and in those early years the "big three" breeds—the Labrador, the golden, and the Chesapeake Bay retriever—competed on a more-or-less equal basis. By the 1950s, however, the Lab's superiority had emerged, and in the years since then it has put even more distance between itself and the competition. A handful of goldens and the occasional Chessie show up to keep things interesting, but for every one of them in a given stake there'll likely be 30 or 40 Labs.

It's not only retrieving ability that makes the Labrador overwhelmingly dominant (although certain Lab partisans may beg to differ) but temperament and trainability. Today's field trial tests are so demanding, and so complex, that to be successful a dog must be trained to a level that was unimaginable a few decades ago. This favors dogs able to withstand a heavy dose of "pressure"—defined by Thomas Quinn, in his classic *The Working Retrievers*, as "the trainer's insistence on task performance through methods of force or implied force." To a greater extent than the other retrieving breeds, the Lab responds positively to pressure, making the necessary corrections without sulking or rebelling. It also tends to catch on a little faster, and while it'd be wrong to characterize the Lab as "all business" its ability to stay focused, whether in training or in the crucible of competition, gives it yet another leg up.

Why Do Labs Love to Pull?

Pulling—which probably stems from the same survival circuitry that causes wild animals to fight against any kind of physical restraint—just comes naturally to dogs. And for almost as long as there have *been* dogs, people have been putting this inclination to their advantage—harnessing it, you might say. Perhaps the first breed mentioned specifically as a draft animal (an animal used to "draw" a load) was the Roman molossus, the large, mastiff-like dog that was also used as a war dog, guard dog, and combatant in gladiatorial spectacles. The molossus is believed to be the taproot of many European work and hunting breeds, including—you guessed it—the St. Hubert's hound, the ancestor of the modern Lab. While the monks at the Abbey of St. Hubert selected their breeding stock primarily on hunting ability, from what we know of monastic life it's inconceivable that they *didn't* put their dogs in harness from time-to-time.

Such informed speculation aside, it's known for a fact that when the St. John's dogs of Newfoundland weren't out with the cod fishing fleet, they were hitched to carts and used to ferry gear between the docks and the watermen's shacks. So when you study the Lab's family tree, you see that there's a long tradition of pulling. Today, of course, Labs pull kids in little red wagons; they pull duck skiffs heaped with decoys across spongy marshlands; they pull the cargo sleds known as *pulks* on winter camping trips; and they pull cross-country skiers, sometimes faster than they care to go, in the wildly exhilirating sport called *skijoring*.

They also pull us along in the slipstream of their infectious *joie de vivre*—and, by their very presence, lighten our emotional load considerably.

Why Do Labs Love Going for Walks?

There are several reasons for this, separate but intertwined. One is that Labs tend to be active, high-energy dogs, and any activity that provides an outlet for that energy—like taking a walk—is bound to be relished. I'm convinced that dogs not only *need* exercise, they're hard-wired to *desire* it. In the wild, where the law of fang and claw remains in force and survival of the fittest is no game, there's a lot to be said for staying in tip-top condition. Evolution, of course, has a way of reinforcing any behavior that contributes to survival by making it feel good, and exercise is no exception.

Another reason Labs love going for walks is that they have an innate curiosity about the world around them. Walking is an opportunity to explore, to take in the sights, sounds, and, most importantly, the smells. Labs are among the most social of dogs, too, so they view walks as a chance to renew old acquaintances, make new ones, and simply stay in circulation. Dogs also like to know what's going on in their environment, and for most Labs in 21st century America, a walk is their primary vehicle for staying informed. Finally, a walk allows your Lab to spend quality time with the alpha member of its pack—you—and for the typical Lab it doesn't get any better than that. This holds true no matter how wretched an excuse for a human being you happen to be, dogs being the only creatures on earth that love us not for who we are, but in spite of what we are.

Why Do Labs Love Riding in Cars and Sticking Their Heads out the Window?

Other than the exercise component, the same reasons that Labs love going for walks explain why they adore riding in cars. It's a chance to get out, explore, and see what's cookin'; plus, it's a chance to spend time with you. It also means *not* being left behind, which all Labs detest and some are positively neurotic about. Even if it's just a trip to the grocery store, your Lab views it as a Great Adventure, fraught with possibility and therefore not to be missed. Even the most laid-back Lab starts prancing like a circus pony when the garage door opens and the car backs out.

There's no mystery whatsoever as to why Labs—all dogs, for that matter—like to stick their heads out the window. Remember, dogs see with their noses, and a dog in a car with the windows rolled up experiences the same kind of sensory deprivation we do in a darkened room. Open the window just a crack, though, and your dog'll wedge its nose into it as far as it'll go, drinking in the aromas, processing a technicolor rush of sensory data. I suppose it's something like watching an IMAX movie, though undoubtedly better.

Why Do Labs Rebel Between One and Two Years Old?

Actually, it can happen as early as five or six months in some individuals. Scary, huh? The short answer, of course, is because at that age your Lab's essentially a teenager and, well, need I say more? Whether human or canine, a teenager is the original Dr. Jekyll/Mr. Hyde. One minute you're smiling beatifically and bragging about your dog's brilliance; the next you're wondering, in a sort of stunned, slack-jawed stupor, what demonic spirit has turned it into a stubborn, willful, unresponsive beast that seems to have forgotten every lesson it ever learned, resists all attempts at further training, and clearly takes a perverse glee in making your life hell. According to animal behaviorist Dr. Patricia McConnell of the "Calling All Pets" public radio program, this is when the (in)famous destructive chewing of Labs typically manifests itself.

What's happening is that your Lab's making the transition from puppyhood to adulthood—and, in true adolescent fashion, asserting its independence by rebelling against you and, more to the point, the authority you represent. Roiling beneath the surface, though, is a corrosive brew of frustration and insecurity that sometimes needs to be vented. And in the same way that your teenager demands to be "treated like an adult"—yet howls at the injustice of being shouldered with adult responsibilities—your teenage Lab is torn between the desires to establish its adult persona and to retain its carefree "puppy priviliges." To use the pop psychology buzzword, it's "conflicted."

Your only conflict, when you catch it shredding your Gucci loafers, will be between the intellectual understanding of the need to stay calm and the emotional urge toward the commission of mayhem.

Why Do Adult Labs Sometimes Refuse Commands?

For the same reasons we humans do, essentially, when we defy our boss, spouse, parent, or similar authority figure: Because to comply would put them in a stressful, disagreeable, or confusing situation. Or—and I'm convinced this is as true of Labs as it is of people—*because they just don't feel like it.* Whether dogs can "think," as we understand the term, remains a hotly debated topic (I believe that they can), but there's no doubt whatsoever that they're capable of many of the mental processes that are the building blocks of thinking, such as weighing alternatives, choosing one course of action over another, and exercising a certain amount of free will. It seems entirely within the realm of possibility that once in a while even the most agreeable of them simply won't be in the mood.

Every dog is an individual, of course, with an individual capacity to assimilate, process, and respond to information. This helps explain why dogs that are highly trained—and thus subject to intense pressure—sometimes "shut down," suddenly refusing commands they've complied with on hundreds of previous occasions. It's their way of telling us they're burned out.

Dogs told to do something they don't want to do typically display an "avoidance behavior" (or "escape behavior"). Retreating to a place where they feel safe and secure—their crate or bed, for example—is probably the most common; others include sitting, lying down, standing stock-still, yawning, sneezing, refusal to make eye contact, and just sort of sniffing around pretending not to hear you. This reminds me of my young nephew, who when his parents tell him something he doesn't want to hear holds up his hand and says "You're talkin' to the hand."

Why Do Labs Sometimes Display Aggression Toward Other Dogs?

Just so we're clear on this, we're not referring to the kind of aggression that occurs when your Lab's backed into a corner by another dog and literally has no choice but to defend itself. That's normal, and excusable. We're talking about *offensive* aggression, about your happy, friendly, well-adjusted Lab going after another dog without provocation or warning. It's completely at odds with the even-keeled Labrador "profile"—and it may be the single most vexing behavioral problem a Lab owner can face.

Diagnosing the root cause (or causes) is often a process of elimination. The first thing to rule out is some underlying physical problem: A dog that suddenly begins acting aggressively may be in pain, and the mere possibility of being bumped or jostled by another dog is enough to set it off. (Injuries involving the spinal column are notorious for this.) On the psychological front, extreme possessiveness regarding its owner—often coupled with feelings of jealous insecurity—can lead to a violent outburst. As Dr. Patricia McConnell puts it, "They view their owner as a giant bone, and their attitude is 'It's mine, and I'm not sharing.'" Dogs with serious fear, territoriality, or dominance issues ("alpha wannabes," McConnell calls them) are also likelier than most to display such behavior; ditto a Lab that's had a traumatic experience with another dog. If the bad news is that there's no quick fix—reaching immediately for the electronic collar, which is the first impulse of many owners, often does more harm than good in these cases—the good news is that aggressive Labs are the ultra-rare exception that simply proves the rule.

Why Are Labs Distrustful of Some Strangers and Not of Others?

Reflecting the breed's abidingly even temperament, Labs in general display great equanimity toward strangers. If they didn't, they wouldn't be the number one choice for guide and service dogs. No matter how level-headed a given Lab may be, however, if it's had an unpleasant experience at the hands of a particular person it's likely to view all physically similar people with suspicion. Labs are capable of astonishing feats, but because reading books is not among them—yet—the covers are what they have to go by.

In other words, Labs do exactly what law enforcement officers are sternly warned not to: They profile. A person may sing in the church choir, volunteer at a homeless shelter, and help little old ladies across the street, but if he happens to resemble a guy who once mistreated your Lab—or even if he uses the same after shave—your Lab's going to keep him in its sights.

In the wild, of course, there's very little survival value in viewing an animal capable of eating you as an individual rather than as a representative of a certain class. Logicians would criticize this as faulty inductive reasoning—reasoning from the part to the whole—but Mother Nature makes her own rules. You can scratch all the lions you want to without finding a lamb. Wolves brought this philosophy with them when they became dogs, which helps explain why you should always let the owner facilitate your introduction to a Lab you've never met. For all you know, you could be a dead ringer for the dog's version of its ex-mother-in-law, the local animal control officer, or whatever form its worst nightmare takes.

Why Do Labs Seem Able to Read Our Minds and Tune In to Our Moods?

One of the hallmarks of the canine race is the ability to tune into our emotional wavelength and give us precisely what we need at a given moment: a frenzied "welcome home"; a soulful, knowing gaze; a reassuring thump of the tail. It shouldn't surprise anyone that Labs are among the most popular therapy dogs, giving comfort to the aged, infirm, and alone, serving as vessels into which men and women subject to the most intense emotional pressures can pour their grief.

The puzzlement has always been *How do they know?* It's not as if they checked our bank balance, read the letter from the doctor, or calculated how long it's been since we had a day off from work. Well, the usual answer is that dogs have a "sixth sense" that enables them to identify our state of mind and respond appropriately. In a way this may be true: Emotional tur-moil is often expressed physiologically, so it seems possible that Labs, with their unimaginably superior powers of olfaction, can sometimes literally smell our moods. What's even more likely, though, is that they're able to pick up on subtle visual signals—posture, carriage, facial expression—that they "decode" to determine our general state of mind. An experiment by Dr. Brian Hare of Harvard showed that dogs have an uncanny ability to correctly interpret these "cues," far better than wolves and even chimpanzees. Hare's conclusion was that there's been "direct selection for dogs with the ability to read social cues in humans"—meaning that for 15,000 years the dogs who were best at interpreting our body language have been the ones kept for breeding.

Which explains why our Labs can read us like a book.

Why Do Labs Eat Grass?

While the statement "All dogs eat grass" is impossible to prove—and while there may be a few Arctic sled dogs that don't eat grass because they live where there's no grass to eat—every dog I've ever known, including every Lab, has been at least an occasional eater of grass. Which is not to be confused with an occasional smoker of grass. (Just don't try to tell me you didn't inhale.) In any event, the $64,000 question has always been: Do dogs get sick and throw up because they eat grass, or do they eat grass because they feel sick and want to throw up? The answer, of course, is "Yes."

The thing you have to remember is that dogs are carnivores by nature, but omnivores by necessity and circumstance. When their wolf forebears brought down a moose, deer, caribou, or any of the large herbivores that were (and are) their preferred prey, they immediately tore into the paunch, consuming not only the flesh and organs but vegetable matter in various states of digestion. Over time, the canine race developed a taste for the stuff—meaning that our Labs' occasional Jonesing for a salad is an atavistic expression of a deeply rooted racial memory. This desire appears strongest in the spring, when the grass is in the first greenly vibrant flush of growth and our Labs, their appetites whetted by a winter of deprivation, are keen for a little grazing. Alas, lacking the necessary enzymes to digest vegetable matter "straight" (not pre-digested, that is), no sooner does the grass go down than it comes back up—at which point *you* start to feel sick.

Why Do Labs Sometimes "Kick" Their Poop After Defecating?

Experienced dog hands always keep a wary eye on any pooch doing its business within a fluidly defined "radius of influence." Depending on the size of the dog, this can be anywhere from a few feet to 15 or 20 yards—the approximate distance, with a generous margin for error, that the dog can propel a semi-solid object by kicking with its hind legs. You can't really call yourself a dog person unless you've had to dive for cover to avoid getting, um, "plastered."

Why do dogs, including Labs, occasionally do this post-defecation kick-step, scratching, digging, and tearing up the turf like a cross between an ornery bull and a neophyte golfer with a nine-iron and a bucket of balls to whack? One theory—again harking back to the struggle for survival faced by the dog's wolf ancestors—holds that dogs kick dirt over their stools in an attempt to make their presence less obvious, both to potential prey species and to the bigger, badder predators a link or two above them on the food chain. Covering their tracks, in other words.

Another theory posits that the purpose is to "spread it around" and leave a scent signature similar to what they do when they "mark" with urine. Then there are those who argue that it's an instinctive "housekeeping" behavior, a way for dogs to police their area—dilution of pollution—and even keep their treads clean, the way we do when we scuff our boots across a stiff-bristled mat. In this same vein, I have a hunch that a few vigorous kicks help to dislodge "cling-ons" and leave the dog feeling minty-fresh. They just look so darn *happy* when they're doing it, so exuberantly gleeful, that it *must* feel good.

Why Do Labs Roll in Offal, Carrion, and Other Vile and Stinky Stuff?

This is one of the most perplexing canine behaviors of all, because on the surface it seems to make so little sense. Knowing how repulsive a bloated roadkill or a carp that floated ashore last week is to us—and knowing how vastly more sensitive the canine sense of smell is than ours—it's hard to reconcile their relish for the rotten. If anything, you'd think they'd give it an even wider berth than we do. *Au contraire*: A lot of very experienced dog people will tell you that the worst offenders in this respect are the dogs with the best noses. The only conclusion that can possibly be reached is that things not only smell *more* to dogs, they also smell *different*—and, for the most part, not too bad.

But if this helps explain why our Labs are so blissfully unperturbed by malodorous dreck that makes us retch, it still begs the question of why they go the extra mile and roll around in it. One theory is that they do it in order to mask their scent and thereby avoid (or at least delay) detection by potential prey species. Not that the typical Lab has to roam the 'burbs hunting for its supper, but in the place where the wolf still howls it doesn't know that. The other theory—the two are not mutually exlusive, by the way—is that they roll in carrion, offal, excrement, and the like as a way to make a record of their travels, a record that other dogs can then "read" and learn from. As Elizabeth Marshall Thomas notes in *The Hidden Life of Dogs*, a dog that's smeared itself with stinky goo is viewed by its brethren as a storyteller, and canine society holds storytellers in high esteem. The person charged with giving this four-legged bard a bath is likely to be less impressed.

Why Do Labs Stick Their Noses in People's Crotches?

As noted earlier, dogs apprehend the world primarily through their noses, *secondarily* through their eyes. When one dog meets another, in particular one it doesn't immediately recognize, it uses its nose to ascertain the stranger's identity. The place it puts its nose to do this, of course, is the rear end—the "inguinal area," if you want to get technical. Every dog has a unique "scent signature" associated with its anal glands, a pair of small, kidney-shaped structures on either side of the anus. Like an olfactory fingerprint (only more revealing), this signature distinguishes it from other dogs, tells whether it's male or female, and is believed to convey additional information as well—although the exact nature of this information remains a mystery, at least to humans.

The long and short of it is that the anatomical nether region, with its bouquet of intriguing aromas, is simply where a dog in search of answers goes. And because the typical well-socialized Lab considers people to be nothing but somewhat eccentric members of its own kind, it perceives no violation of etiquette or decorum in planting its wet, cold nose right in our front yard. Think of it as the dog's way of saying "Hello… Have we been introduced?" It's also the case that the muzzle of the average Lab and the crotch of the average person happen to occupy approximately the same level, meaning there's a certain amount of "locational inevitability" at work, too.

Why Do Labs Beg for Food?

Because (A) no self-respecting Lab *ever* passes up a chance to eat and (B) we let them. In fact, we encourage them, feeling the press of a muzzle (or, more likely, the insistently repeated nudge) against our thigh and, when we think no one's looking, slipping them a tidbit under the table. It's yet another example of something we've already referenced, the positive feedback loop: Your Lab sits next to your chair, gazing at you imploringly and doing its best to impersonate poor, pathetic, half-starved Oliver Twist. You fall for it—not that it's much of a drop—and *voila!* a morsel of steak magically finds its way from your plate to your Lab's mouth. The behavior thus reinforced in what must seem to your Lab a spectacularly gratifying way, it starts the act all over again.

The problem is that it's all too easy to let this seemingly innocent little game get out of hand. It's like smoking the occasional cigarette: Before you know it, you've developed a pack-a-day habit. Labs are the most obesity-prone breed in America (there are statistics that back this up); if their diet isn't carefully monitored in relationship to the amount of exercise they receive, that layer of fat that insulates them against the cold turns into a blubbery spare tire. An overweight dog is at risk for the same litany of health problems an overweight person is: diabetes, cardiovascular disease, joint and skeletal deterioration, et. al. So while slipping your Lab a morsel of "people food" now and then is fine, too much of a good thing isn't.

Why Do Some Labs Point?

We've all seen wild predators, wolves being the obvious example, stalk prey. Their gaze unwavering, their movements so fluid you'd swear a glass of water would balance on their backs, they advance in a series of stealthy stops-and-starts. This stop, when the predator "freezes" to avoid alerting and prematurely flushing the prey—you can even see it in a great blue heron stalking minnows at the edge of a lake—is believed to be the taproot of the point as we know it today: the dog a living statue, tail rigid, one forepaw raised as it "points" to the location of the hidden pheasant, quail, or other gamebird. In the bona fide pointing breeds—the pointer, the Brittany, the various setters—the desire to point has been refined via centuries of selective breeding into the dominant and definitive characteristic.

Most Labs, in contrast, will instinctively charge in and flush any gamebirds they detect. And most sportsmen are happy to have them do so. A few Labs, however, have always displayed some degree of "point," even if it's nothing more than that momentary hesitation (often called a "flash point") hard-wired into the predatory genes. But by breeding one Lab with a pronounced inclination to point to another, and repeating this process for several generations, there are now established "lines" of pointing Labrador retrievers. The rationale is that by adding pointing to the repertoire of the dog acknowledged to be the retriever *par excellence*, you get the best of both worlds. A lot of people—a lot of serious Lab breeders in particular—don't buy it, and in fact argue that it's detrimental. That's the word they use in polite company, anyway.

Why Do Labs Dig Holes and Bury Bones?

On a pound-for-pound basis, the Lab never lived that was a match for a really feisty terrier in the digging department. The name "terrier," after all, derives from the Latin word for earth, *terra*, and in antiquity terriers were in fact known as "earth dogges." But because Labs are big, strong animals, they're capable of doing serious damage—to the yard, vegetable garden, flower bed, pretty much any surface you can think of that yields, crumbles, or otherwise gives way to their steam-shovel front paws. A Lab of a mood to dig, its entire expression so glassily intent and oblivious to everything else that its mind seems to have temporarily slipped its moorings, can sling dirt with the best of them.

The reason Labs dig is that, like so many of the behaviors we've discussed, it proved useful to their wolf forebears in the struggle for survival and therefore became part of the genetic blueprint for the entire *Canis* genus. It enabled them to root out prey from their underground (or under-snow) burrows, to excavate dens for puppy whelping and rearing, and to simply create a cool, comfortable spot to lie down. It also enabled them to "cache" surplus food for later consumption—which is what our Labs are doing when they bury bones. Again, while they probably don't have to fret over when and where their next meal's coming from, there's a part of them that isn't so sure.

The good news is that, given their druthers, there's a lot of stuff Labs would rather do than dig. It's when they're bored and have nothing better to do, typically, that the digging instinct rears its destructive head.

Why Do Labs Bark and Sometimes Howl?

One of the more interesting ways dogs and wolves differ is that while wolves *can* bark, they almost never *do*. In light of this, canine ethologists have theorized that, like the ability to "read" our body language, humans cultivated this behavior in the domesticated dog because it proved useful to them. A dog that barked when it detected a saber-toothed tiger prowling the edges of the encampment was a valuable commodity, and as the barkers were rewarded by being allowed to breed the behavior became an integral part of the make-up of *Canis lupus familiaris*. From the gritty urban alleyways to the Chem-lawned 'burbs, wherever there are dogs there's the cacophony of barking.

These days, while Labs still bark to sound the alarm and issue a challenge to intruders, they also bark at other dogs (and sometimes their toys) as an invitation to play, out of sheer exuberance, and out of grinding boredom. They bark, too, when they're trying to tell us something. "Grandma locked herself in the bathroom again," for example. Dogs having figured out long ago that we're not nearly as good at intepreting *their* body language as they are at interpreting ours (to say nothing about decoding their scent signals), barking is perhaps their primary means of communicating with us. Would that we were better at undertanding them.

As for howling, which wolves use to communicate a range of information as well as simply to proclaim their emotional state, it's not especially common among Labs. When they do indulge, it's often in response to the wail of a siren—a siren they'll hear several seconds before you do. If your Lab starts howling for no apparent reason, just wait.

Why Do Labs Spend So Much Time Napping?

Unlike many of their owners (at least those with American addresses) Labs aren't obsessed with being "productive." This may seem paradoxical, given that no breed comes remotely close to the Lab in terms of the sheer quantity of work it performs as a hunter, field trial competitor, guide and service dog, etc. But what it really reflects is the Lab's psychologically healthy, "to everything there is a season" attitude. When there are no more ducks to be fetched or bags to be sniffed or city streets to be negotiated, the typical, well-adjusted Lab is perfectly content to wile away the hours in Dreamland (which, as we've seen, is for dogs a sort of virtual reality amusement park). Assuming their engagement calendar's clear, a nap (or two) will likely be at the top of the day's agenda.

It's worth remembering that, as Elizabeth Marshall Thomas notes in *The Hidden Life of Dogs*, dogs relish the opportunity to "do nothing." If you think about how difficult the struggle for survival is in the wild—and recall how little-changed the dog is, fundamentally, from the wolf—you begin to grasp the nap's larger significance. What a treat to be able to steal a few moments of blissful, untroubled, deliciously restorative sleep! It's one of life's great pleasures—and, like the next meal, its availability is never, ever taken for granted. Give a Lab a job to do, and it'll happily work itself to the nub. Give a Lab the day off, though, and it emulates Dagwood Bumstead and makes a beeline for the sofa.

Why Do Labs Love Us Despite Our Faults?

Earlier I made the observation that the dog has given man the chance to play God, molding, shaping, and sculpting the various breeds to satisfy our needs, suit our fancies, and, in the case of the Lab, embody a vision of perfection. I even stated that we've made the dog in our own image—but on second thought that's not quite right. In fact, we've made the dog (and the Lab in particular) *better*, endowing it with the qualities that we like to believe we possess but, being all too human, typically fall short in: courage, loyalty, devotion, selflessness, patience, perseverance, good humor, an astonishing capacity to forgive, ad. inf. Their example shames us.

If there is a single defining quality, however, it is the fierce, abiding, unconditional love our Labs give us, a love so profound that its depths remain utterly unfathomed, utterly mysterious. Sometimes, gazing into their dark, knowing eyes—eyes that look at us as if we can do no wrong—we feel as if we can see all the way to the bottom of their souls. But then, when we're sure they have nothing left, they find a way to give more—and they leave us stunned. We wonder *Where does it come from? What have we done to deserve it?*, and we search in vain for an answer. Perhaps it is enough simply to appreciate it, to recognize it for the great gift, the incomparable blessing, that it is.

Why Do Labs Risk Their Lives to Save Their Masters?

The lore and literature of dogdom is replete with tales of canine courage, heroism, and selflessness: dogs that pulled people from the wreckage of burning buildings; dogs that body-blocked children out of the path of speeding cars; dogs that battled violent intruders even after they themselves suffered terrible wounds. It's often said that dogs put themselves in harm's way because they have no foreknowledge of death; they sense that their master needs help and, ignorant of the potential consequences, they respond. There's certainly a germ of truth in this—but it's equally true that dogs, like all sentient beings, have an extraordinarily powerful survival instinct. Sometimes, when you consider the evidence, the only reasonable conclusion is that they're fully aware they're putting their life on the line. The fact that they do it willingly, without hesitation, only serves to underscore their inherent—but lightly worn—nobility.

Labs are not unique in this respect—it's one of the hallmarks of the entire canine race—but I have a hunch that the same qualities that make them the number one choice for guide and service work (including the physical "tools") predispose them toward these acts of heroism. Their devotion to us is so complete, and so uncompromising, that when they sense we're in danger they literally can't help but respond. No Lab owner is ever in doubt that his dog would take a bullet for him.

We can't hope to measure up to that standard—but we owe it to our Labs to try.

Photo credits